Great Explorers

By James Buckley Jr.

Editor Radhika Haswani
Senior Art Editor Ann Cannings
Art Editors Shubham Rohatgi, Roohi Rais
Jacket Coordinator Francesca Young
Jacket Designers Dheeraj Arora, Amy Keast
DTP Designers Dheeraj Singh, Vikram Singh
Picture Researcher Deepak Negi
Producer, Pre-Production Rob Dunn
Producer Niamh Tierney
Managing Editors Deborah Lock, Monica Saigal
Managing Art Editor Diane Peyton Jones
Deputy Managing Art Editor Ivy Sengupta
Art Director Martin Wilson
Publisher Sarah Larter
Publishing Director Sophie Mitchell

Reading Consultant Jacqueline Harris
Subject Consultant Lyles Forbes
The Mariners' Museum and Park, Newport News, VA, USA

First published in Great Britain in 2018
by Dorling Kinderslely Limited
80 Strand, London, WC2R 0RL

The publisher would like to thank the following for their kind permission to reproduce their photographs:
(Key: a-above; b-below/bottom; c-centre; f-far; l-left; r-right; t-top)
1 Alamy Stock Photo: Mikael Utterström. **3 Dorling Kindersley:** Tina Chambers / National Maritime Museum, Greenwich, London (br). **4 Dorling Kindersley:** James Stevenson / National Maritime Museum, London (cra). **6 Dorling Kindersley:** James Stevenson / National Maritime Museum, London (cra). **7 Alamy Stock Photo:** Rafael Ben-Ari. **10-11 Getty Images:** Imagno (b). **12-13 Alamy Stock Photo:** World History Archive (b). **13 Dreamstime.com:** Gennady Poddubny / Poddubnygennady (tr). **14-15 Alamy Stock Photo:** Mikael Utterström. **14 Dorling Kindersley:** James Stevenson / National Maritime Museum, London (cra). **16-17 Science Photo Library:** Library of Congress, Geography and Map Division. **17 Dorling Kindersley:** James Stevenson / National Maritime Museum, London (tr). **18 Dorling Kindersley:** Ruth Jenkinson / Holts Gems (br); Tim Parmenter / Natural History Museum, London (cb). **19 Getty Images:** DEA / M. Seemuller. **20 Dorling Kindersley:** Tina Chambers / National Maritime Museum, Greenwich, London (cra); James Stevenson / National Maritime Museum, London (c, clb). **21 Dorling Kindersley:** James Stevenson / National Maritime Museum, London (tl); Whipple Museum of History of Science, Cambridge (br). **22 Dorling Kindersley:** Alan Hills / The Trustees of the British Museum (br); James Stevenson / National Maritime Museum, London (cra). **23 Alamy Stock Photo:** GL Archive. **24 Getty Images:** Mansell. **25 123RF.com:** wrangel (br). **26-27 Alamy Stock Photo:** Chronicle. **28-29 Getty Images:** Underwood Archives (b). **30 Getty Images:** Bettmann (bl). **31 Courtesy of Centre for Newfoundland Studies, Memorial University Libraries:** Mina Hubbard Collection / Archives and Special Collections / Queen Elizabeth II Library (tr). **Getty Images:** Apic (cl). **Library of Congress, Washington, D.C.:** (br). **32 Dorling Kindersley:** James Stevenson / National Maritime Museum, London (cra). **33 Getty Images:** Bettmann. **35 Alamy Stock Photo:** Granger Historical Picture Archive. **36-37 Getty Images:** Bates Littlehales / National Geographic (t). **38 NASA. 39 NASA:** (cb). **40-41 NASA:** JPL-Caltech / University of Wisconsin. **40 123RF.com:** Galyna Andrushko (cl). **41 123RF.com:** BlueOrange Studio (cra); dinozzaver (crb). **NASA:** JPL-Caltech / MSSS (tl). **43 Dorling Kindersley:** James Stevenson / National Maritime Museum, London (br)
Jacket images: *Front:* **Getty Images:** Bettmann; *Back:* **123RF.com:** Ilya Sharapov bl
Endpaper images: *Front:* **Getty Images**: *DEA / M. Seemuller* ; *Back:* **Getty Images:** *DEA / M. Seemuller*
All other images © Dorling Kindersley
For further information see: www.dkimages.com

A WORLD OF IDEAS:
SEE ALL THERE IS TO KNOW

www.dk.com

Contents

What is out there?

"What is out there?" Humans have been asking that question for thousands of years. Some people seek new places. They seek to discover new things or to become rich. They seek adventure. These people are explorers.

Exploring can be about testing yourself.

Chapter 1
Early
explorations

The first explorers were sailors
more than 4,000 years ago.
Polynesians (pah-leh-NEE-shuns)
explored the huge Pacific Ocean.
They followed the stars to guide
their way. They also
watched where
birds flew and how
the winds blew.
They found many
islands where they
could live.

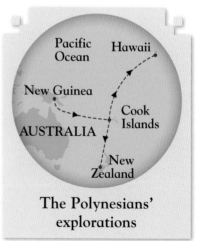

The Polynesians'
explorations

The Polynesians tied together a pair of canoes to make a large sailing canoe.

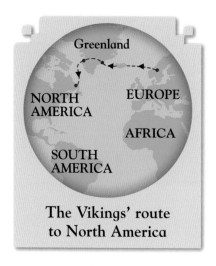

The Vikings' route
to North America

The Norsemen, or Vikings, from northern Europe were explorers about 1,200 years ago. They explored to find gold, silver and other treasures. They also sailed to other lands to find good places to live.

Some Vikings sailed across to Greenland and North America. A few of them set up homes there.

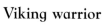

Viking warrior

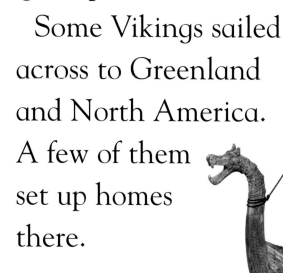

Sail

Viking longships were made from wood.

Oar

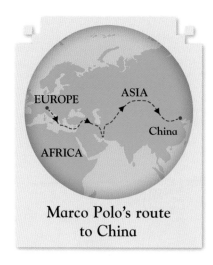

Marco Polo's route
to China

Not all early explorers went by ship. Marco Polo travelled overland from Venice in 1260. He went to China and back again. He was seeking new places to buy and sell things.

Marco Polo travelled with horses and camels.

Marco later visited many parts of Asia. He wrote a book about the amazing places he saw.

Marco Polo bought silk from China.

Making maps

People needed a way to record the location of places. They made maps so that other people could visit the places.

Muslim mapmaker Muhammad al-Idrisi (ul-id-REE-si) made this map in 1154.

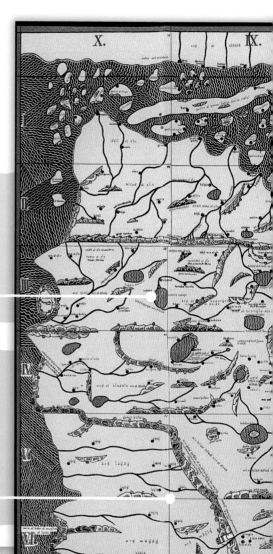

Al-Idrisi showed how maps could include lots of information.

An ancient Roman, Ptolemy (TALL-uh-mee), first used the grid system on maps.

Many old maps show
sea monsters in
unknown parts
of the ocean.
Mapmakers wrote,
"Here there
be dragons!"

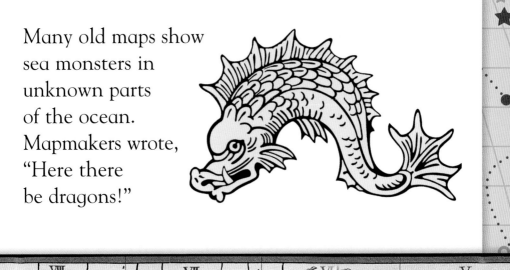

Chapter 2
Age of exploration

In the 1400s, the Europeans went to look for new places in the world. They found new routes across the oceans. Christopher Columbus was an Italian explorer. He headed west from Spain in 1492. He thought he would reach India. Instead he reached the Caribbean islands!

Columbus's ships were called *Santa Maria*, *Niña* and *Pinta*.

NORTH
AMERICA   EUROPE

Atlantic
Ocean   AFRICA

SOUTH
AMERICA

**Christopher Columbus's
route in 1492**

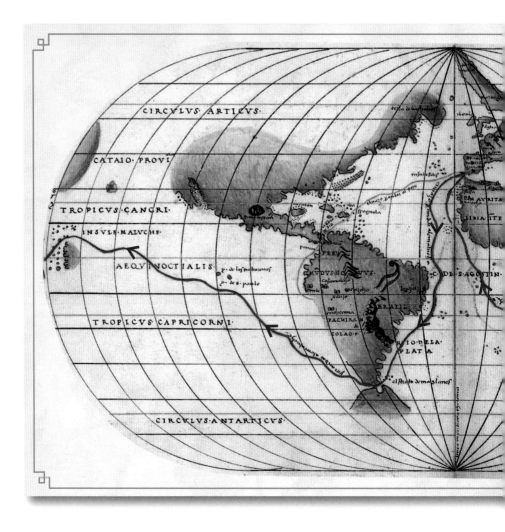

Ferdinand Magellan set out
from Spain in 1519. He had
five ships and 270 sailors.
They sailed around the southern
point of South America.

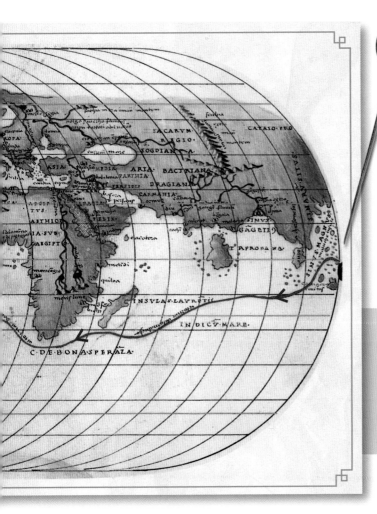

Map dividers were used to measure distances on a map or chart.

This map shows the route of Magellan's ships around the world.

Europeans had sailed only as far as the Pacific Ocean. Magellan's ships sailed on around the world. Only 18 sailors came back. Magellan was not one of them.

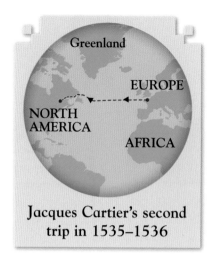

Greenland

EUROPE

NORTH AMERICA

AFRICA

Jacques Cartier's second trip in 1535–1536

Jacques Cartier (Car-TEE-A) sailed to North America in 1534. He was sent by the French king. He explored the St. Lawrence River in Canada on his second trip. He searched for silver, gold, diamonds, copper and spices. He did not find any even on his third trip there.

Cartier looked for these valuable gems and minerals.

Diamond

Silver

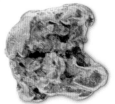

Gold nugget

Cartier gave Canada
its name.

Navigation tools

Early explorers used special tools to help them find their way.

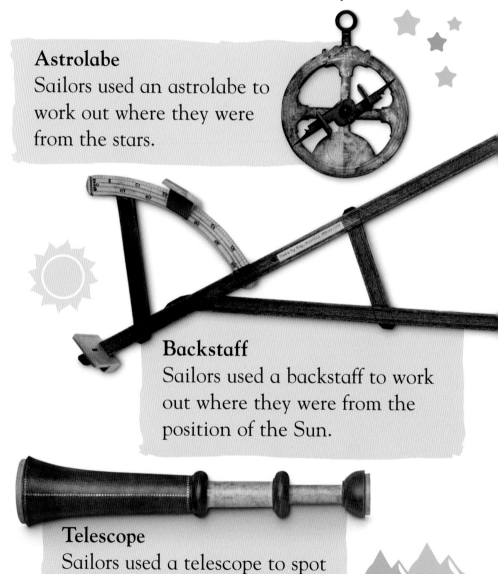

Astrolabe
Sailors used an astrolabe to work out where they were from the stars.

Backstaff
Sailors used a backstaff to work out where they were from the position of the Sun.

Telescope
Sailors used a telescope to spot land from far away.

Compass
A compass always shows which way is north.

Chronometer
Sailors used this special ship clock to tell the time.

Chapter 3
Exploring continents

Explorers had sailed around most of the world by the 1700s. Now people wondered what the lands were like.

A British sea captain named James Cook reached Australia in 1770. He also explored New Zealand and the Pacific Islands. Europeans had never seen most of them before.

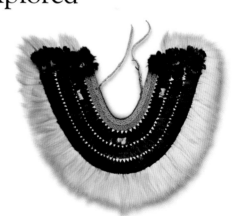

Chest ornament
from Tahiti

Pacific
Ocean

Cook
Islands

AUSTRALIA

New
Zealand

Part of James Cook's
first voyage

James Cook made maps
of the Pacific Ocean.

Lewis and Clark look towards the Rocky Mountains.

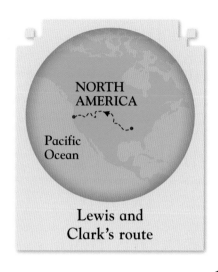

NORTH AMERICA

Pacific Ocean

Lewis and Clark's route

Meriwether Lewis and William Clark were from eastern United States of America. They were sent to explore the west in 1804. They led 31 men and one dog on this trip. They travelled on flatboats, horses and by foot. They finally reached the Pacific Ocean in 1805. They had help on the way from a Native American woman, Sacagawea (Sacka-juh-WEE-uh).

Sacagawea on a US dollar coin

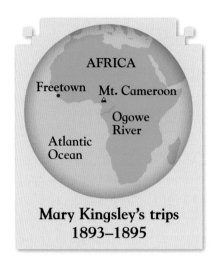

AFRICA

Freetown   Mt. Cameroon

Ogowe
River

Atlantic
Ocean

**Mary Kingsley's trips
1893–1895**

The huge continent of Africa was home to millions of native people. Europeans had hardly seen any of this continent.

Mary Kingsley travels along the Ogowe River.

Between 1893 and 1895, British explorer Mary Kingsley went to West Africa. She met the people and found new animals. She faced a leopard and fought off a crocodile.

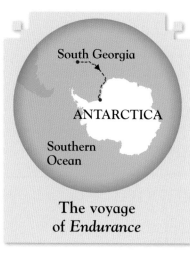

South Georgia

ANTARCTICA

Southern
Ocean

The voyage
of *Endurance*

Ernest Shackleton
explored Antarctica.
He went on his third
trip there in 1914.

His ship was called *Endurance*.
It became stuck in the ice.
   Shackleton and his crew were
trapped for over a year. He led a
team across the Antarctic to find
help. He finally saved his crew.

Crew member exercises
one of the dog teams.

READY FOR ADVENTURE!

Many people in the past thought women should not explore. But women were brave travellers, too.

Around the World in 72 Days!

1889
Writer Nellie Bly circled the globe by ship, train, balloon and other transport.

Lure of the Wild

1905

Mina Benson Hubbard led an expedition into unknown wilderness in Canada.

The Queen of the Desert

1921

Gertrude Bell went to the Middle East to map the places and meet the people.

Reaching new Heights

1906

Fanny Bullock Workman was the first to climb to the top of Pinnacle Peak in the Himalayas, Asia.

Chapter 4
Modern
exploration

Explorers in modern times find new challenges. Some explorers take to the air. Amelia Earhart was the first woman to fly on her own across the Atlantic Ocean in 1932. She also flew across the USA and back again. She went missing when she flew over the Pacific Ocean in 1937.

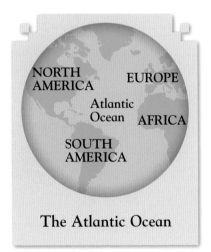

The Atlantic Ocean

Amelia Earhart was
an American pilot.

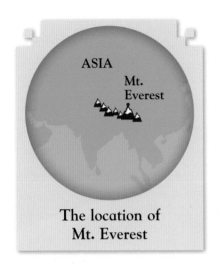

The location of
Mt. Everest

Some explorers try to reach the top of the world. Mt. Everest is the highest mountain in the world.

Sir Edmund Hillary was a British explorer. Tenzing Norgay was from the Sherpa people of Nepal. They were the first climbers to reach the top in 1953. More than 4,000 climbers have done the same since then.

Hillary and Norgay near
the summit of Mt. Everest

Some people say we have
explored only a tiny part
of the oceans. Sylvia Earle
is an American scientist.

ASIA

NORTH
AMERICA

Pacific
Ocean

AUSTRALIA

SOUTH
AMERICA

The Pacific Ocean

Sylvia Earle studies
a seaweed.

She dives deep underwater
all around the world. Her
discoveries show how important
the oceans are to us all.

Buzz Aldrin walks
on the moon.

What is beyond Earth? Humans started exploring space in the 1960s. Neil Armstrong and Buzz Aldrin were astronauts. They landed on the moon in 1969.

Today astronauts live on the International Space Station. More than 200 people have visited there since 2000. They are from many countries.

Sandra Magnus on the International Space Station

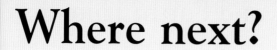

Where next?

People seek new places
to explore today and
in the future.

Caves

There are underground and
underwater caves still to be found.

Mars

People are building spacecraft that they hope will take people to the planet Mars.

Oceans

There are still many unknown parts of the deep ocean.

Mountain forests

There are some wild and hard to reach places still to explore.

Quiz

1 Which part of the world did the Polynesians explore?

2 Which explorer travelled overland from Venice in 1260?

3 How many ships and sailors did Ferdinand Magellan set sail with in 1519?

4 Who did the French king send out to explore North America in 1534?

5 What is the special ship clock called?

6 Name the Native American who helped Meriwether Lewis and William Clark on their trip.

7 Who took his third trip to Antarctica in 1914?

8 In which year did Amelia Earhart fly on her own across the Atlantic Ocean?

9 Which American scientist dives deep under the ocean all around the world?

10 In which year did Neil Armstrong and Buzz Aldrin land on the moon?

Answers on page 45

Glossary

adventure
exciting activity

ancient
very long time ago

canoe
light, narrow boat with pointed ends

continent
large area of land

crew
people who work together on a ship

discoveries
places or objects that are found

expedition
journey to explore

explore
find out about something new

fleet
group of ships

globe
world

grid
lines that cross each other to make squares

native
person born in a particular place

navigate
stay on course to get from place to place

overland
on land

route
course to get from place to place

solo
alone

wilderness
area of land with no or few people

Answers to the quiz:

1. Pacific Ocean; 2. Marco Polo;
3. Five ships and 270 sailors; 4. Jacques Cartier;
5. Chronometer; 6. Sacagawea; 7. Ernest
Shackleton; 8. 1932; 9. Sylvia Earle; 10. 1969

Guide for Parents

DK Readers is an exciting four-level reading series for children that will help to develop the habit of reading widely for both pleasure and information. These chapter books have an engaging main narrative to suit your child's reading ability, interspersed with additional information spreads in a range of reading genres. Each book is designed to develop your child's reading skills, fluency, grammar awareness and comprehension in order to build confidence and pleasure in reading.

Ready for a *Beginning to Read* book

YOUR CHILD SHOULD

- be using phonics, including consonant blends, such as br, sp and st, to sound out unfamiliar words; and be familiar with common word endings, such as plurals, ing, ed and ly.
- be using the meaning of the text, the grammar of a sentence plus clues from the illustrations to check and correct his/her own reading.
- be pausing briefly at commas, and for longer at full stops; and altering his/her expression for question, exclamation and speech marks.

A VALUABLE AND SHARED READING EXPERIENCE

For many children, reading requires a lot of effort, but adult participation can make this both fun and easier. So here are a few tips on how to use this book with your child.

TIP 1 Check out the contents together before your child begins:

- read the text about the book on the back cover.
- read through and discuss the contents page together to heighten your child's interest and expectation.
- have a brief discussion about unfamiliar or difficult words on each page.
- chat about the non-fiction reading features used in the book, such as headings, captions and labels.

TIP 2 Support your child as he/she reads each page:

- give the book to your child to read and turn the pages.

- where necessary, encourage your child to break a word into syllables, sound out each one and then flow the syllables together. Ask him/her to reread the sentence to check the meaning.

- you may need to help read some topic-related vocabulary and other words that may be difficult for your child.

- when there's a question mark or an exclamation mark, encourage your child to vary his/her voice as he/she reads the sentence. Demonstrate how to do this if it is helpful.

TIP 3 Praise, share and chat:

- the additional information spreads are designed to be shared and discussed with your child. These spreads tend to be more difficult than the main narrative.

- ask your child questions about the meaning of the text and of the words used. This will help to develop comprehension skills and awareness of the language used.

A FEW ADDITIONAL TIPS

- Encourage your child to try reading difficult words by themselves. Praise any self-corrections, for example, "I like the way you sounded out that word and then changed the way you said it to make sense."

- Try to read together every day. Reading little and often is best. These books are divided into manageable chapters for one reading session. However, after 10 minutes, only keep going if your child wants to read on.

- Read a variety of books of different types with your child for pleasure and information. Reading aloud to your child is a great way to develop his or her reading skills!

- Make reading an enjoyable experience for your child.

Index